MUFFINS &
QUICK BREADS

MUFFINS & QUICK BREADS

IRENA CHALMERS

LONGMEADOW PRESS

The recipes contained in this book have been tested and tried. However, results may vary depending on the conditions in your kitchen.

STAFF FOR NO NONSENSE COOKING GUIDES

EDITORIAL DIRECTION: Jean Atcheson

MANAGING EDITOR: Mary Goodbody

COVER DESIGN: Karen Skelton

ART DIRECTION & DESIGN: Helene Berinsky

RECIPE DEVELOPMENT: Elizabeth Wheeler, Ruth Arthur

ASSISTANT EDITOR: Maurice Goodbody

COVER PHOTOGRAPH: Matthew Klein

TYPESETTING: ComCom, Allentown, Pennsylvania

CONTENTS

ACKNOWLEDGMENT

Grateful acknowledgment is made to Dudley-Anderson-Yutzy for permission to reproduce or adapt original recipes.

MUFFINS & QUICK BREADS

L ifting a pan of freshly baked muffins or a warm loaf of quick bread from a hot oven is a happy chore. The sight of the muffins or bread cooling on the kitchen counter evokes good, comfortable feelings of home and serenity. Finally, eating the fruits of your labor and watching your family and friends enjoy them are hugely rewarding. With this book these pleasures will be yours. We will guide you through the steps of making perfect, high-domed muffins, chunky quick breads, sweet coffee cakes and delicate tea cakes. Never again will you run to the baker or rely on packaged products when you feel the need for something "baked" to round out the meal.

Nearly all our recipes require double-acting baking powder and baking soda to raise them. The baking powder is a mixture of an alkali (generally bicarbonate of soda) and an acid (calcium acid phosphate) which, when moistened, reacts to form carbon dioxide, the gas which raises the batter. This leavening is further activated by heat, which is why the muffins or breads rise to the most astonishing heights in the oven. In some

7

recipes, where an acidic ingredient such as molasses, buttermilk or yogurt is included, the recipe may call for baking soda alone, an alkali that will react to the acid. More often, however, baking soda is added to the recipe to neutralize the acid ingredient while baking powder is relied on to supply the lion's share of the leavening.

For the most part, our recipes call for room-temperature ingredients. Milk, eggs and butter are meant to be taken from the refrigerator 20 to 30 minutes before baking to give them ample time to lose their chill. When all the ingredients, dry and liquid, are the same temperature, they blend together better and produce a more satisfactory batter. When the butter is melted, it should be cooled before being added to the batter. If a recipe calls for melted butter, you might consider melting it in the microwave. It is fast and easy and often the container you use can be washed in the dishwasher, while a butter melting pan may require hand washing.

Rarely is it necessary to use an electric mixer when making muffins or quick breads. Instead, the ingredients are mixed with a sturdy wooden spoon or rubber spatula by a dozen or so quick strokes. They should be stirred just until the dry and liquid ingredients are combined and the batter is no longer streaky. There is no need to worry if there are a few lumps in the batter— they will disappear during baking. Ingredients such as nuts and fruit usually are added at the end of mixing and should be incorporated with three or four brisk strokes.

We have varied the size of the muffin cups in the recipes that follow. Most are for the standard six- or seven-tablespoon-sized cups. A few recipes call for mini muffin tins or jumbo ones. Any muffin batter can be baked in large, small or standard-sized muffin cups, but the baking time will have to adjusted. If, for instance, you decide to make mini savory cheese muffins to serve with cocktails and our recipe has instructions for large muffins, simply watch the little muffins carefully and check them for doneness after 10 or 12 minutes of baking. They may need more time—and you can tell this by sticking a toothpick into the center of one to see how wet the batter inside is—but at least you can begin watching the muffins carefully at this point, checking them every few minutes. The opposite is true for giant muffins; they require longer baking.

With muffins and quick breads, we suggest letting them cool in the pan for five or 10 minutes before turning them out on a wire rack to cool completely. Otherwise, the muffins or breads may fall apart if they are removed from the pan as soon as it is taken from the oven. However, if you let the muffins or breads sit in the pan too long, their bottoms will turn soggy from lack of air circulating to cool them properly.

Almost all the ingredients called for are available in supermarkets. Some may be easier to find in specialty shops or your own garden. Although we do not always specify, it is advisable to rinse all fruits and vegetables and peel all fruits, such as apples and pears. Use firm, ripe fruits and vegetables, neither too immature nor overripe. A bruise here and there matters not at all, unless it is an indication that the fruit is past its prime.

This assortment of muffins, quick breads, coffee cakes, tea cakes and sweet and savory spreads is designed to meet all needs for these quick and easy baked wonders. Whether you want to indulge in a rich, sweet chocolate chip muffin or munch on a slice of healthful carrot loaf, you will find something here to fulfill your desires and satisfy your cravings for something home-baked.

CHAPTER 1

MUFFIN BASICS

This book begins with a primer on muffins—everybody's favorite breakfast treat. But in today's grab-something-good-to-eat-and-run-out-the-door world, muffins have gone way beyond breakfast and are turning up in lunch boxes, brown bags, desk drawers, glove compartments and beach bags. Most people instantly think of bran, corn and blueberry when they think "muffins," which prompted us to include prototype recipes for these classics in this chapter. Bake them a few times and you will be more than ready to tackle some of the more exotic recipes in later chapters.

We have also included some information on substituting ingredients in basic recipes to "customize" your muffins. You can make them sweeter, less sweet, more nutty tasting (by adding whole wheat flour, for example) and richer. You will quickly learn that muffins are simple to make—and even simpler to eat! And you will be rewarded every time you produce a version that suits your own particular taste preferences.

Corn Muffins

Makes 12 muffins

What is more classic, when it comes to muffins, than a hot, crumbly corn muffin? Here is the best recipe we have run across in a long time.

> *1 cup all-purpose flour*
> *1 cup yellow cornmeal*
> *¹/₃ cup sugar*
> *1 tablespoon baking powder*
> *¹/₂ teaspoon salt*
> *1 cup milk, at room temperature*
> *8 tablespoons (4 ounces) butter,*
> * melted and cooled*
> *2 large eggs, at room temperature*
> *1¹/₂ teaspoons vanilla extract*

We tested these recipes using unsalted butter; they can equally well be made with lightly salted butter.

Heat the oven to 400 degrees. Lightly butter twelve 2⁷/₈-by-1³/₈-inch (7 tablespoon) muffin cups.

Stir together the flour, cornmeal, sugar, baking powder and salt. In another bowl stir together the milk, butter, eggs and vanilla. Make a well in the center of the flour mixture, add the milk mixture and stir just to combine. Spoon the batter into the prepared muffin cups.

Bake for 15 to 20 minutes until a toothpick inserted in the center of one muffin comes out clean. Remove the tin(s) to a wire rack. Cool for 5 minutes before removing the muffins from the cups. Serve warm or finish cooling on the rack.

Bran Muffins

Makes 32 muffins

Do you fancy a bran muffin for breakfast? Or maybe a quick and healthy afternoon snack? With this super batter in the refrigerator, you can quickly bake one or more muffins any time you want to—no mixing, no fussing. The batter will keep refrigerated in an airtight container for as long as two weeks. Of course, if you prefer, you can bake the muffins as soon as you mix the batter; cut the baking time back by five minutes or so if the batter is *not* chilled. The recipe yields a lot of batter, so you might choose to bake a batch of muffins right away and refrigerate the rest for later.

When a recipe calls for both oil and molasses, measure the oil first. Use the same measuring cup, without rinsing it, for the molasses, and it will slip right out. This works with honey and syrup, too.

> 5 cups bran cereal, such as All-Bran or Bran
>   Buds
> 1 1/2 cups unprocessed bran
> 4 cups buttermilk, at room temperature
> 6 large eggs, at room temperature
> 12 tablespoons (6 ounces) butter,
>   melted and cooled
> 1/2 cup vegetable oil
> 1/2 cup molasses
> 1 teaspoon vanilla extract
> 1 cup packed brown sugar
> 5 1/2 cups all-purpose flour
> 1 tablespoon baking powder
> 2 teaspoons baking soda
> 1 1/2 teaspoons salt

Heat the oven to 400 degrees. Lightly butter the desired number of 2 7/8-by-1 3/8-inch (7 tablespoon) muffin cups.

Stir together the bran cereal and bran, stir in the buttermilk and let stand until the buttermilk is absorbed. In another bowl stir together the eggs, butter, oil, molasses and vanilla. Stir in the brown sugar and then the bran mixture. In a very large bowl stir together the flour, baking powder, baking soda and salt. Make a well in the center of the flour mixture, add the liquid mixture and stir just to combine. Transfer the batter to an airtight container and chill for up to 2 weeks.

When ready to bake, spoon ⅓ cup of the chilled batter into each prepared muffin cup. Bake for 22 to 27 minutes until a toothpick inserted in the center of one muffin comes out clean. Remove the tin(s) to a wire rack. Cool for 5 minutes before removing the muffins from the cups. Serve warm or cool completely on the rack.

A VARIATION

Using batter from the refrigerator, stir about 1 cup of chopped dried fruit or nuts into 4 cups of batter just before baking for added flavor and texture. Do not overmix the batter when incorporating these additional ingredients.

FREEZING MUFFINS

After they have been allowed to cool completely, muffins freeze very well. Wrap them in foil and stow them in the freezer for a rainy day. Reheat them by unwrapping the foil and then rewrapping it loosely around the muffins. Heat frozen muffins for 15 to 20 minutes at 350 degrees. Room-temperature or chilled muffins reheat in 5 to 10 minutes at 250 degrees.

Blueberry Muffins

Makes 12 muffins

Blueberry muffins have justly earned the reputation of being an American tradition. For the best tasting, most appealing muffins, use freshly picked summer berries.

> 2 cups all-purpose flour
> 1 cup sugar
> 1 teaspoon baking powder
> 1 teaspoon baking soda
> 1/2 teaspoon salt
> 1/2 cup plain low-fat yogurt, at room
>   temperature
> 1/3 cup orange juice, at room temperature
> 4 tablespoons (2 ounces) butter,
>   melted and cooled
> 1 large egg, at room temperature
> 1 1/2 teaspoons vanilla extract
> 1/4 teaspoon grated orange rind (optional)
> 2 cups fresh blueberries, rinsed and drained

Heat the oven to 400 degrees. Lightly butter twelve 2 5/8-by-1 1/8 (6 tablespoon) muffin cups.

Stir together the flour, sugar, baking powder, baking soda and salt. In another bowl stir together the yogurt, orange juice, butter, egg, vanilla and orange rind, if desired. Make a well in the center of the flour mixture, add the yogurt mixture and stir just to combine. Stir in the blueberries. Spoon the batter into the prepared muffin cups.

Bake for 20 to 25 minutes until a toothpick inserted in the center of one muffin comes out clean. Remove the tin(s) to a wire rack. Cool for 5 minutes before removing the muffins from the cups. Serve warm or cool completely on the rack. These muffins freeze particularly well.

SUBSTITUTING INGREDIENTS

(in recipes producing 10 to 12 standard-sized muffins)

- Depending on the measure of all-purpose flour, you can substitute the equivalent amount of whole wheat flour or cornmeal, or replace half the all-purpose flour with whole wheat flour or cornmeal.

- To fortify a recipe with unprocessed bran, wheat germ or rolled oats, substitute $1/2$ cup of these for up to $1/2$ cup of the flour specified in the recipe. In other words, if the recipe calls for $1\frac{1}{2}$ cups of flour, use 1 cup of flour and $1/2$ cup of bran, wheat germ or rolled oats.

- When making muffins, you can reduce the amount of sugar to as little as 2 tablespoons for a savory muffin. (Try this with corn muffins, for example.) For sweeter muffins, increase the measure of sugar to $1/2$ cup if, for instance, the recipe calls for $1/4$ or $1/3$ cup of sugar.

- An equal amount of tightly packed brown sugar can be substituted for the measure of granulated sugar. For instance, $1/2$ cup of packed brown sugar replaces $1/2$ cup of granulated sugar. Use dark or light brown sugar; there is almost no difference in taste.

- With a little trial and error, you can replace part of the measure of sugar with honey or molasses. When using these sweeteners in amounts larger than 2 tablespoons, consider them liquid ingredients and reduce the rest of the liquid accordingly.

- Increase the amount of shortening by $1/4$ cup for richer muffins. However, for recipes requiring no more than 1 cup of flour and 1 egg, the quantity of shortening should not exceed 8 tablespoons (4 ounces).

- Margarine is an acceptable alternative to butter but do not expect the same rich flavor.

- You can replace the vanilla extract with an equal measure of almond or maple extract. Simply adding $1/4$ teaspoon of almond or maple extract to a recipe calling for 1 teaspoon of vanilla extract will produce a more subtly flavored muffin.

CHAPTER 2

SWEET MUFFINS

A napkin-lined basket of hot, freshly baked muffins on the morning table is a joyous sight to sleepyheads and early risers alike. Even before the first cup of coffee is poured, eager hands will reach under the colorful napkin to bring forth a warm, deliciously fragrant, sweet muffin. When the shadows lengthen and it is time for tea, muffins are most welcome with a strong, hot cup. And after a light lunch of a sandwich or soup, a muffin satisfies a sweet tooth far better than a candy bar.

In this chapter, we have included muffins chock-full of chocolate chips, tasty dried fruit, buttery nuts, zesty citrus fruit, and moist bananas and pumpkin puree. Sweetened with granulated and brown sugar and baked to a golden turn, each makes as good a dessert as a breakfast bread. Try them with spreads, sweet butter or unadorned—and simply splendid.

Jumbo Fruit and Nut Chocolate Bar Muffins

Makes 6 jumbo muffins

Pack one of these mega muffins in your child's lunch box and he may ask to go to school on Saturday! After all, who can resist a giant muffin with a chopped-up candy bar baked right in it? You can always have some on hand because these muffins freeze very well indeed.

> 2 cups all-purpose flour
> 1/2 cup packed brown sugar
> 1/4 cup sugar
> 2 teaspoons baking powder
> 1/2 teaspoon salt
> 2/3 cup milk, at room temperature
> 8 tablespoons (4 ounces) butter, melted and cooled
> 2 large eggs, at room temperature
> 2 teaspoons vanilla extract
> 2 5-ounce milk chocolate, raisin and almond bars, cut into 1/2-inch pieces

Many recipes suggest filling muffin cups no more than half or two-thirds full, but the muffins will have a higher dome if the cups are filled nearly to the brim—leave a little leeway, though.

Heat the oven to 375 degrees. Lightly butter six 3 1/4-by-1 3/8-inch (2/3 cup) muffin cups.

Stir together the flour, sugars, baking powder and salt. In another bowl combine the milk, butter, eggs and vanilla. Make a well in the center of the flour mixture, add the milk mixture and stir just to combine. Stir in the chocolate bar pieces. Spoon the batter into the prepared muffin cups.

Bake for 25 to 30 minutes until a toothpick inserted in the center of one muffin comes out clean. Remove the tin to a wire rack and cool for 5 minutes before removing the muffins from the cups. Finish cooling on the rack and serve warm or completely cool.

Mini Banana Date Nut Muffins

Makes 24 miniature muffins

These little "bites" of sweet muffins are ideal for the tea table, or earlier, with coffee and juice.

> 2 cups all-purpose flour
> 1/4 cup sugar
> 1/4 cup packed brown sugar
> 1 1/2 teaspoons baking powder
> 1/4 teaspoon baking soda
> 1/4 teaspoon salt
> 1 cup mashed ripe bananas, about 2 large
>   bananas
> 8 tablespoons (4 ounces) butter,
>   melted and cooled
> 2 large eggs, at room temperature
> 1/3 cup buttermilk, at room temperature
> 1 1/2 teaspoons vanilla extract
> 1 cup chopped dates
> 1 cup chopped walnuts

Chocolate lovers can substitute chocolate chips for the dates. And, of course, you can use any combination of dried fruit and nuts. Whatever your choice, the muffins freeze well.

Heat the oven to 375 degrees. Lightly butter twenty-four 1 3/4-by-7/8-inch (2 tablespoon) muffin cups.

Stir together the flour, sugars, baking powder, baking soda and salt. In another bowl combine the bananas, butter, eggs, buttermilk and vanilla. (The mixture will look curdled.) Make a well in the center of the dry ingredients, add the banana mixture and stir just to combine. Stir in the dates and walnuts. Spoon the batter into the prepared muffin cups.

Bake for 20 to 25 minutes until a toothpick inserted in the center of one muffin comes out clean. Remove the tin(s) to a wire rack and cool for 5 minutes before removing the muffins from the cups. Finish cooling on the rack and serve warm or completely cool.

Peanut Butter Cup Muffins

Makes 12 muffins

What a surprise! Nestled inside each of these sweet muffins is a soft, warm chocolate cup filled with peanut butter.

> 2 1/4 cups all-purpose flour
> 2/3 cup packed brown sugar
> 1 tablespoon baking powder
> 1/4 teaspoon salt
> 3/4 cup milk, at room temperature
> 2/3 cup chunky-style peanut butter
> 1/3 cup vegetable oil
> 2 large eggs, at room temperature
> 2 teaspoons vanilla extract
> 12 bite-sized peanut butter-filled chocolate cups

Heat the oven to 400 degrees. Lightly butter twelve 2 7/8-by-1 3/8-inch (7 tablespoon) muffin cups.

Stir together the flour, sugar, baking powder and salt. In another bowl whisk together the milk, peanut butter, oil, eggs and vanilla until combined. Make a well in the center of the dry ingredients, add the milk mixture and stir just to combine. Spoon a heaping tablespoon of the batter into each muffin cup. Press a peanut butter cup into the center of the batter. Spoon the remaining batter over the tops of the cups, making sure that the candies are completely covered.

Bake for 15 to 20 minutes until the tops are lightly browned and the muffins feel "set." Remove the tin(s) to a wire rack. Cool for 5 minutes before removing the muffins from the cups and finish cooling on the rack. Serve warm or completely cool.

Chocolate Chip Muffins

Makes 12 muffins

Everyone loves chocolate chip cookies; now we can indulge in this all-American taste treat with muffins. Try these with milk and white chocolate chips, or a combination of all three. Make plenty and freeze them for whenever the chocolate urge strikes.

> 2 cups all-purpose flour
> 1/2 cup honey crunch wheat germ
> 1/3 cup packed brown sugar
> 1/3 cup sugar
> 2 teaspoons baking powder
> 1/4 teaspoon salt
> 3/4 cup milk, at room temperature
> 8 tablespoons (4 ounces) butter,
>   melted and cooled
> 2 large eggs, at room temperature
> 1 1/2 teaspoons vanilla extract
> 1 1/2 cups semisweet chocolate chips
> 3/4 cup chopped pecans

Heat the oven to 400 degrees. Lightly butter twelve 2⁷/₈-by-1³/₈-inch (7 tablespoon) muffin cups.

Stir together the flour, wheat germ, sugars, baking powder and salt. In another bowl combine the milk, butter, eggs and vanilla. Make a well in the center of the flour mixture, add the milk mixture and stir just to combine. Stir in the chocolate chips and pecans. Spoon the batter into the prepared muffin cups.

Bake for 15 to 20 minutes until the tops are lightly browned and the muffins feel "set." Remove the tin(s) to a wire rack. Cool for 5 minutes before removing the muffins from the cups and finish cooling on the rack. Serve warm or completely cool.

Apricot White Chocolate Muffins

Makes 12 muffins

The tart-sweet flavor of the dried apricots offsets the sweetness of the white chocolate in these crunchy, nut-filled muffins.

> 2 cups all-purpose flour
> 1/3 cup packed brown sugar
> 1/3 cup sugar
> 2 teaspoons baking powder
> 1/4 teaspoon salt
> 2/3 cup milk, at room temperature
> 8 tablespoons (4 ounces) butter,
>   melted and cooled
> 2 large eggs, at room temperature
> 1 1/2 teaspoons vanilla extract
> 1 cup chopped dried apricots
> 6 ounces white chocolate, cut into 1/4-inch pieces
> 3/4 cup coarsely broken walnuts

Heat the oven to 400 degrees. Lightly butter twelve 2 7/8-by-1 3/8-inch (7 tablespoon) muffin cups.

Stir together the flour, sugars, baking powder and salt. In another bowl combine the milk, butter, eggs and vanilla. Make a well in the center of the flour mixture, add the milk mixture and stir just to combine. Stir in the apricots, chocolate and walnuts. Spoon the batter into the prepared muffin cups.

Bake for 20 to 25 minutes until the tops are lightly browned and the muffins feel cooked when touched. Remove the tin(s) to a wire rack. Cool for 5 minutes before removing the muffins from the cups and finish cooling on the rack. Serve warm or completely cool.

You can insert pleated paper cups in the muffin tins rather than buttering them. The liners look pretty and save time, too.

Oatmeal Raisin Muffins

Makes 8 muffins

The old-fashioned goodness of oatmeal and raisins comes through in grand style in these wonderful muffins. Try them for breakfast or brunch—or later in the day.

> 1 1/4 cups all-purpose flour
> 3/4 cup uncooked old-fashioned rolled oats
> 1/2 cup sugar
> 2 1/2 teaspoons baking powder
> 1/4 teaspoon salt
> 1/2 cup milk, at room temperature
> 1/3 cup (2 2/3 ounces) butter,
>   melted and cooled
> 1 large egg, at room temperature
> 1 1/2 teaspoons vanilla extract
> 3/4 cup raisins

Fill any unused cups in the tin with water before baking the muffins. This prevents the tin from warping in a hot oven and insures even baking because the cups do not get overly hot, which could cause the batter in adjoining cups to cook too quickly.

Heat the oven to 400 degrees. Lightly butter eight 2 7/8-by-1 3/8-inch (7 tablespoon) muffin cups. Fill any unused cups with water.

Stir together the flour, oats, sugar, baking powder and salt. In another bowl combine the milk, butter, egg and vanilla. Make a well in the center of the flour mixture, add the milk mixture and stir just to combine. Stir in the raisins. Spoon the batter into the prepared cups.

Bake for 15 to 20 minutes until a toothpick inserted in the center of one muffin comes out clean. Remove the tin(s) to a wire rack and cool for 5 minutes before removing the muffins from the cups. Finish cooling on the rack and serve warm or completely cool.

Lemon Nut Muffins

Makes 12 muffins

With a sweet crumb topping, delicately perfumed with lemon, these tender, tangy muffins are as welcome for afternoon tea as they are for breakfast.

MUFFINS:
1 3/4 cups all-purpose flour
1 cup chopped pecans or walnuts
1/3 cup packed dark brown sugar
2 teaspoons baking powder
2 teaspoons grated lemon rind
1/2 teaspoon salt
1 large egg, at room temperature
1/2 cup milk, at room temperature
6 tablespoons (3 ounces) butter,
  melted and cooled
1/4 cup sour cream, at room temperature

TOPPING:
3 tablespoons all-purpose flour
3 tablespoons sugar
2 teaspoons grated lemon rind
2 tablespoons (1 ounce) butter, softened

Grate lemon or orange rind to take off the colored part of the skin only, avoiding any of the bitter white pith.

Heat the oven to 400 degrees. Lightly butter twelve 2 7/8-by-1 3/8-inch (7 tablespoon) muffin cups.

To make the muffins, stir together the flour, chopped nuts, sugar, baking powder, lemon rind and salt in a bowl. In another bowl beat the egg and stir in the milk, melted butter and sour cream. Make a well in the flour mixture, add the milk mixture and stir just to combine. Spoon the batter into the prepared muffin cups.

Combine the topping ingredients, mixing with a fork until the mixture is crumbly and thoroughly blended. Sprinkle the topping evenly over the muffin batter.

(continued)

Bake for 20 to 25 minutes until a toothpick inserted in the center of one of the muffins comes out clean. Remove the muffins to a wire rack to cool in the tin(s) for 5 minutes. Turn the muffins out of the cups. Serve warm.

Pumpkin Muffins with Pumpkin Seeds

Makes 12 muffins

When the autumn winds blow chill and the "frost is on the pumpkin," curl up in front of a toasty fire with a batch of these moist, delicious muffins, satisfyingly crunchy because of a judicious measure of pumpkin seeds in the batter and sprinkled on top.

Pumpkin seeds
are available at
health food
stores—and the
canned pumpkin
provides a
healthy amount of
vitamin A.

2 cups all-purpose flour
3/4 cup packed brown sugar
2 teaspoons baking powder
1/4 teaspoon baking soda
1/2 teaspoon salt
1 teaspoon cinnamon
1/4 teaspoon powdered ginger
1/8 teaspoon ground cloves
Dash ground nutmeg
1 cup canned pumpkin
1/3 cup (2 2/3 ounces) butter,
    melted and cooled
2 large eggs, at room temperature
1/4 cup buttermilk, at room temperature
2 teaspoons vanilla extract
1 cup plus 2 tablespoons pumpkin seeds

Heat the oven to 400 degrees. Lightly butter twelve 2⅞-by-1⅜-inch (7 tablespoon) muffin cups.

Stir together the flour, sugar, baking powder, baking soda, salt, cinnamon, ginger, cloves and nutmeg. In another bowl combine the pumpkin, butter, eggs, buttermilk and vanilla. Make a well in the center of the dry ingredients, add the pumpkin mixture and stir just to combine. Stir in 1 cup of the pumpkin seeds. Spoon the batter into the prepared muffin cups and sprinkle the remaining seeds on top of the muffins.

Bake for 15 to 20 minutes until a toothpick inserted in the center of one muffin comes out clean. Remove the tin(s) to a wire rack and cool for 5 minutes before removing the muffins from the cups. Finish cooling on the rack and serve warm or completely cool.

FLAVORING ADD-ONS

Any number of "extras" can be added to sweet muffins and quick breads for flavor and texture. Try, when the recipe seems appropriate, grated citrus rind, vanilla or almond extract, ground cinnamon, chopped dried fruit or butterscotch chips. Adjust the amounts according to the recipe.

CHAPTER 3

SAVORY MUFFINS

When the day is done and supper weighs on your mind, think about mixing up a batch of easy, savory muffins. Nothing will please your family more than just-baked corn muffins or tangy Italian muffins. As with all muffins, these take only minutes to mix, a half hour or so to bake and a few minutes to cool—which means that in the time it takes to heat a casserole or stew and toss a salad, you can set oven-fresh muffins on the table.

We have devised a number of full-bodied muffins flavored with robust cheeses and meats, heady herbs and rich nuts. Any one of them will round out a weekday supper or make a weekend meal very special indeed. They all make wonderful snacks, too, for those times when you want to nibble food that has good, honest flavor without being too filling. Savory muffins are right on target.

Cheddar Cheese Muffins

Makes 12 muffins

Dashes of spicy mustard and Tabasco bring out the rich, bright flavor of cheddar in these tasty muffins. Just right for an afternoon snack or served alongside soup and salad.

> 2 cups all-purpose flour
> 1 1/2 tablespoons sugar
> 1 1/2 teaspoons baking powder
> 1/2 teaspoon baking soda
> 1/8 teaspoon salt
> 1 cup grated extra-sharp cheddar cheese
> 1 cup buttermilk, at room temperature
> 1/3 cup (2 2/3 ounces) butter,
>   melted and cooled
> 1 large egg, at room temperature
> 1 teaspoon prepared spicy brown mustard
> 1/8 teaspoon Tabasco sauce

Heat the oven to 400 degrees. Lightly butter twelve 2 5/8-by-1 1/8-inch (6 tablespoon) muffin cups.

Stir together the flour, sugar, baking powder, baking soda and salt. Stir in the cheese. In another bowl combine the buttermilk, butter, egg, mustard and Tabasco. Make a well in the center of the flour mixture, add the buttermilk mixture and stir just to combine. Spoon the batter into the prepared muffin cups.

Bake for 15 to 20 minutes until a toothpick inserted in the center of one muffin comes out clean. Remove the tin(s) to a wire rack. Cool for 5 minutes before removing the muffins from the cups. Serve warm.

Muffins that contain cheese or meat should be refrigerated if they are not eaten right away.

Vegetable Muffins

Makes 12 muffins

On a cool September evening, gather some fresh zucchini and pull a carrot or two from the garden to make these tantalizing muffins.

¹/₃ cup (2²/₃ ounces) butter
¹/₂ cup shredded zucchini
¹/₂ cup shredded carrot
¹/₃ cup thinly sliced scallions, including green tops
1 teaspoon finely chopped garlic
2 cups all-purpose flour
2 teaspoons baking powder
1¹/₂ teaspoons sugar
¹/₂ teaspoon salt
¹/₂ teaspoon baking soda
1 cup buttermilk, at room temperature
1 large egg, at room temperature

If you bake these in miniature muffin cups, they make smashing hors d'oeuvres.

Heat the oven to 400 degrees. Lightly butter twelve 2⅝-by-1⅛-inch (6 tablespoon) muffin cups.

Heat the butter in a skillet until melted. Add the zucchini, carrot, scallions and garlic and cook for 1 to 2 minutes until the vegetables are crisp-tender. Remove the pan from the heat and cool for 10 minutes. Stir together the flour, baking powder, sugar, salt and baking soda. In another bowl combine the buttermilk and egg and then stir in the vegetables. Make a well in the center of the dry ingredients, add the buttermilk mixture and stir just to combine. Spoon the batter into the prepared muffin cups.

Bake for 15 to 20 minutes until a toothpick inserted in the center of one muffin comes out clean. Remove the tin(s) to a wire rack. Cool for 5 minutes before removing the muffins from the cups. Serve warm.

Italian Muffins

Makes 9 muffins

A hint of garlic and oregano, the good salty taste of Parmesan and the mellow flavor of ripe olives combine to make as aromatic a muffin as you will ever eat.

1/3 cup (2 2/3 ounces) butter
1 teaspoon finely chopped garlic
3/4 teaspoon dried basil
1/4 teaspoon dried oregano
1/8 teaspoon dried red pepper flakes
2 cups all-purpose flour
1/3 cup grated Parmesan cheese
2 teaspoons sugar
1 tablespoon baking powder
1/4 teaspoon salt
1/2 cup milk, at room temperature
2 large eggs, at room temperature
2/3 cup sliced, pitted ripe olives

Heat the oven to 400 degrees. Lightly butter nine 2 5/8-by-1 1/8-inch (6 tablespoon) muffin cups. Fill any unused cups with water.

Heat the butter, garlic, basil, oregano and red pepper flakes in a skillet until the butter is melted and the garlic has just started to brown. Remove the pan from the heat and cool for 10 minutes. Stir together the flour, Parmesan, sugar, baking powder and salt. In another bowl combine the milk and eggs and then stir in the melted butter mixture. Make a well in the center of the flour mixture, add the milk mixture and stir just to combine. Stir in the olives.

Bake for 15 to 20 minutes until a toothpick inserted in the center of one muffin comes out clean. Remove the tin(s) to a wire rack. Cool for 5 minutes before removing the muffins from the cups. Serve warm.

These taste good with minestrone or other vegetable soup or as a snack at any time of day.

Blue Cheese Walnut Muffins

Makes 12 muffins

The flavor combination of blue cheese and walnuts is hard to beat. These muffins are excellent on the dinner table; make them mini muffin size to serve with cocktails—and watch them disappear.

> 2 cups all-purpose flour
> 1 tablespoon sugar
> 2 teaspoons baking powder
> 1/8 teaspoon salt
> 3/4 cup milk, at room temperature
> 1/3 cup (2 2/3 ounces) butter,
>   melted and cooled
> 1 large egg, at room temperature
> 1/8 teaspoon Tabasco sauce
> 1 cup coarsely crumbled blue cheese
> 3/4 cup chopped walnuts

Grated hard cheese, such as cheddar or Swiss, can be stirred into muffin batter. Use between 2 and 4 ounces for a normal-sized recipe (10 or 12 muffin yield).

Heat the oven to 400 degrees. Lightly butter twelve 2 5/8-by-1 1/8-inch (6 tablespoon) muffin cups.

Stir together the flour, sugar, baking powder and salt. In another bowl combine the milk, butter, egg and Tabasco. Make a well in the center of the flour mixture, add the milk mixture and stir just to combine. Stir in the blue cheese and walnuts. Spoon the batter into the prepared muffin cups.

Bake for 15 to 20 minutes until a toothpick inserted in the center of one muffin comes out clean. Remove the tin(s) to a wire rack. Cool for 5 minutes before removing the muffins from the cups. Serve warm.

Cajun Corn Muffins

Makes 12 muffins

Try these mildly spicy muffins with thick, rich gumbo or fiery chili.

1 1/2 cups yellow cornmeal
1 1/2 cups all-purpose flour
2 tablespoons sugar
1 tablespoon baking powder
1/2 teaspoon baking soda
1/4 teaspoon salt
1 1/3 cups buttermilk, at room temperature
8 tablespoons (4 ounces) butter,
    melted and cooled
3 large eggs, lightly beaten
2 teaspoons prepared spicy brown mustard
1/8 teaspoon Tabasco sauce
3/4 cup (4 ounces) 1/4-inch pieces cooked ham
1 cup finely chopped green and/or red pepper
1/2 cup thinly sliced scallions, including
    green tops

The best cornmeal is stone ground, preferably from a small mill. Store it in the refrigerator.

Heat the oven to 400 degrees. Lightly butter twelve 2 7/8-by-1 3/8-inch (7 tablespoon) muffin cups (and the edges around the cups, if you are using a tin).

Stir together the cornmeal, flour, sugar, baking powder, baking soda and salt. In another bowl combine the buttermilk, butter, eggs, mustard and Tabasco. Make a well in the center of the dry ingredients, add the buttermilk mixture and stir just to combine. Stir in the ham, peppers and scallions.

Bake for 20 to 25 minutes until a toothpick inserted in the center of one muffin comes out clean. Remove the tin(s) to a wire rack. Cool for 5 minutes before removing the muffins from the cups and finish cooling on the rack. Serve warm.

Bacon Cheddar Corn Muffins

Makes 10 muffins

Serve these them with a steaming tureen of homemade pea soup or perhaps as part of a light supper, accompanying a quick omelette.

> *8 slices bacon, sliced crosswise into $^1/_2$-inch*
> *   pieces*
> *$^3/_4$ cup cornmeal*
> *$1^1/_4$ cups all-purpose flour*
> *2 teaspoons baking powder*
> *$^1/_2$ teaspoon baking soda*
> *$^1/_2$ teaspoon salt*
> *$1^1/_2$ cups buttermilk, at room temperature*
> *2 large eggs, at room temperature*
> *1 cup grated cheddar cheese*

Heat the oven to 400 degrees. Lightly butter ten $2^5/_8$-by-$1^1/_8$-inch (6 tablespoon) muffin cups. Fill any unused cups with water.

Cook the bacon slowly over low heat until it is crisp. Drain the pieces, reserving 4 tablespoons of the fat, and set aside.

Sift together the cornmeal, flour, baking powder, baking soda and salt. In another bowl combine the buttermilk and eggs, beat well with a fork and add to the dry ingredients. Add the reserved bacon fat and mix just until the dry ingredients are moistened. Fold in the cheese and bacon.

Spoon the batter into the prepared muffin cups. Bake for about 15 minutes until the muffins are well risen and browned and a toothpick inserted in the center of one muffin comes out clean. Remove the tin(s) to a wire rack. Cool for 5 minutes before removing the muffins from the cups. Serve warm.

Onion-Stuffed Muffins

Makes 12 muffins

Light, classic muffins filled with a mild mixture of on-
ions are tasty for lunch or dinner, particularly when the
main course is simply cooked meat or grilled chicken.

4 tablespoons (2 ounces) butter
1 1/2 cups finely chopped onion
1 1/2 cups buttermilk, at room temperature
1 egg, at room temperature
2 1/2 cups all-purpose flour
1 1/2 teaspoons baking soda
3/4 teaspoon salt

Heat the oven to 400 degrees. Lightly butter twelve
2 1/2-inch muffin cups.

Heat 1 tablespoon of the butter in a saucepan. Add
the onion and cook for 5 minutes until softened. Remove the onion from the pan and set aside. Heat the
remaining butter until it is melted.

Combine the buttermilk, egg and melted butter in a
bowl. In another, quite large bowl stir together the
flour, baking soda and salt. Make a well in the flour
mixture, add the buttermilk mixture and stir just to
combine.

Spoon about 1 1/2 tablespoons of batter into each
prepared cup. Top each with 1 1/2 teaspoons of the
reserved onion. Top each muffin equally with the remaining batter. Bake for 25 to 30 minutes until the
muffins are golden brown and a toothpick inserted in
the center of one muffin comes out clean. Remove the
tin(s) to a wire rack. Cool for 5 minutes before removing the muffins from the cups. Serve warm.

Try adding 1/2
teaspoon or so of
your favorite dried
herb to give the
muffin batter
another flavor
dimension.

Nebraska Corn Muffins

Makes 12 muffins

Corn muffins are almost as familiar to a midwestern farm table as a pitcher of cold, foaming milk. These, bolstered by whole kernels of corn, burst with good corn flavor.

> *1 cup all-purpose flour*
> *1 cup yellow cornmeal*
> *2 tablespoons sugar*
> *2 1/2 teaspoons baking powder*
> *1 teaspoon salt*
> *1 cup milk, at room temperature*
> *1/2 cup vegetable oil*
> *2 eggs, at room temperature, lightly beaten*
> *1/2 teaspoon Tabasco sauce*
> *1 cup fresh or frozen corn kernels*

Heat the oven to 400 degrees. Lightly butter twelve 3-by-1 1/4-inch (7 tablespoon) muffin cups.

Stir together the flour, cornmeal, sugar, baking powder and salt. In another bowl combine the milk, oil, eggs and Tabasco. Make a well in the center of the dry ingredients, add the milk mixture and stir just to combine. Stir in the corn.

Spoon the batter into the prepared muffin cups. Bake for 15 to 20 minutes until a toothpick inserted in the center of one muffin comes out clean. Remove the tin(s) to a wire rack. Cool for 5 minutes before removing the muffins from the cups. Serve warm.

CHAPTER 4

QUICK BREADS

Quick breads are delightful to make. The batter takes minutes to mix up and the bread is baked in an hour or so. As they bake, the kitchen fills with the wonderful aromas of baking bread, tantalizing every member of the family with the promise of good things to eat. The basic sweet batter takes kindly to all sorts of added ingredients such as berries, nuts, chopped dried or fresh fruit, chopped vegetables and exotic spices. Similar to muffins in composition, quick breads rise with the aid of baking powder and/or baking soda; their texture and appearance is akin to muffins, too. They have slightly raised tops, which usually are a little cracked, and an uneven crumb.

Called quick breads because they are certainly "quicker" to make than yeast-raised breads, they also derive their name from the way they are mixed. As soon as the dry and liquid ingredients are combined, the leavening action begins and the sooner the bread is popped in the oven, the better it will be. This does not mean you must fly around the kitchen at breakneck speed. But it does mean that the oven should be heated

35

and the pan prepared before the batter is mixed. Work steadily and carefully—and if the telephone rings just as you are scraping the batter into the pan, ask the caller to wait a moment while you put the bread in the oven. Do not leave it sitting on the counter for any length of time. The delicious results are worth this little bit of extra care.

California Fruit and Nut Quick Breads

Makes 8 mini loaves

These tiny loaves, loaded with the good fruits and nuts of the Golden State, are a nice alternative to larger ones. It is a good idea to bake all eight, eat a few, and freeze the rest for later in the month when you need something sweet, delicious and nutritious to tuck in your child's lunch box or to pack with a thermos of coffee for an early-morning car trip.

3 cups all-purpose flour
3/4 cup granulated sugar
1/4 cup packed brown sugar
2 teaspoons baking powder
3/4 teaspoon baking soda
1/2 teaspoon salt
1 cup plain low-fat yogurt, at room temperature
12 tablespoons (6 ounces) butter,
 melted and cooled
2 large eggs, at room temperature
1 1/2 teaspoons vanilla extract

¹/₄ teaspoon grated orange rind
¹/₂ cup chopped dried apricots
¹/₂ cup chopped dates or golden raisins
¹/₂ cup raisins
¹/₃ cup unsalted pistachios
¹/₃ cup chopped walnuts
¹/₃ cup chopped almonds

Heat the oven to 400 degrees. Lightly butter eight 4¹/₂-by-2³/₈-by-1¹/₂-inch (1 cup) miniature loaf pans.

Stir together the flour, sugars, baking powder, baking soda and salt. In another bowl combine the yogurt, butter, eggs, vanilla and orange rind. Make a well in the center of the flour mixture, add the yogurt mixture and stir just to combine. Stir in the dried fruits and nuts. Turn the batter into the prepared pans and smooth the tops of the loaves.

Bake for 30 to 35 minutes until a toothpick inserted in the center of one loaf comes out clean. Remove the pans to a wire rack. Cool for 10 minutes before removing the loaves from the pans. Cool completely on the rack.

Pistachio nuts are naturally green in buff-colored shells. The red-shelled ones are dyed and usually salted—neither is recommended for our recipe.

COOLING QUICK BREADS

Quick breads must be cooled completely before they are sliced; otherwise they will crumble. If you prefer them warm, let them cool and then toast a slice or two. If you plan to freeze the loaves, it is especially important that they be quite cold before being wrapped in heavy foil and frozen.

Plum-Almond Quick Bread

Makes one 8-by-4-inch loaf

Plum delicious!

> *8 tablespoons (4 ounces) butter, softened*
> *3/4 cup sugar*
> *2 large eggs, at room temperature*
> *1 teaspoon vanilla extract*
> *1/4 teaspoon almond extract*
> *1/4 teaspoon grated lemon rind*
> *2 cups all-purpose flour*
> *1/2 teaspoon baking soda*
> *1/4 teaspoon salt*
> *1/2 cup lemon-flavored low-fat yogurt, at room*
>   *temperature*
> *1 cup chopped fresh plums*
> *1 cup slivered almonds*

Heat the oven to 325 degrees. Lightly butter and flour an 8 3/8-by-4 3/8-by-2 5/8-inch loaf pan.

Cream the butter and sugar together until the mixture is light and fluffy. Add the eggs one at a time, beating well after each addition. Beat in the vanilla and almond extracts and the lemon rind.

In another bowl stir together the flour, baking soda and salt. Beat half the yogurt into the butter mixture until smooth, then half the flour mixture. Repeat the process with the rest of the yogurt and the remaining flour mixture. Stir in the plums and almonds. Turn the batter into the prepared pan and smooth the top of the batter.

Bake for 60 to 70 minutes until a toothpick inserted in the center of the loaf comes out clean. Remove to a wire rack. Cool the bread in the pan for 15 minutes. Remove the bread from the pan and cool completely on the rack.

Tropical Bread

Makes one 8-by-4-inch loaf

Buttery macadamia nuts and golden papaya invest this loaf with some warm island magic.

> 8 tablespoons (4 ounces) butter, softened
> 1/3 cup granulated sugar
> 1/3 cup packed brown sugar
> 2 large eggs, at room temperature
> 1 cup mashed ripe bananas, about 2 large bananas
> 1/4 cup milk
> 2 teaspoons vanilla extract
> 2 cups all-purpose flour
> 1 teaspoon baking powder
> 1/2 teaspoon baking soda
> 1/4 teaspoon salt
> 1 cup chopped macadamia nuts
> 1 cup chopped dried papaya

Heat the oven to 350 degrees. Lightly butter and flour an 8⅜-by-4⅜-by-2⅝-inch loaf pan.

Cream the butter and sugars together until the mixture is light and creamy. Add the eggs one at a time, beating well after each addition. Combine the bananas, milk and vanilla in a bowl. In another bowl stir together the flour, baking powder, baking soda and salt. Beat half the banana mixture and half the flour mixture into the butter-egg mixture just until combined. Repeat with the remaining banana mixture and the rest of the flour mixture. Stir in the nuts and papaya. Turn the batter into the prepared pan and smooth the top.

Bake for 70 to 80 minutes until a toothpick inserted in the center of the loaf comes out clean. Remove the pan to a wire rack. Cool for 15 minutes before removing the bread from the pan. Cool completely on the rack.

Zucchini Bread

Makes one 9-by-5-inch loaf

The zucchini in this all-American favorite quick bread leaves the loaf tasting especially moist and fresh.

$1/2$ cup raisins
2 cups all-purpose flour
$1/2$ cup packed light brown sugar
1 tablespoon baking powder
1 teaspoon salt
$1/2$ teaspoon ground nutmeg
$1/2$ cup finely chopped walnuts
2 large eggs, at room temperature
$1/2$ cup buttermilk, at room temperature
$1/3$ cup vegetable oil
$1/2$ pound zucchini, coarsely chopped,
    about 2 cups

Heat the oven to 350 degrees. Lightly butter a 9-by-5-inch loaf pan.

Toss the raisins in a bowl with 2 tablespoons of the flour. In another bowl stir together the rest of the flour, brown sugar, baking powder, salt, nutmeg and walnuts.

In another bowl beat the eggs with the buttermilk and oil. Stir in the zucchini and raisins. Make a well in the center of the dry ingredients, add the buttermilk mixture and blend well. Turn the batter into the prepared pan.

Bake for 1 hour until a toothpick inserted in the center of the bread comes out clean. Remove the pan to a wire rack. Cool for 10 minutes before removing the bread from the pan. Cool completely on the rack.

Cranberry Nut Bread

Makes one 9-by-5-inch loaf

Christmas is the season to bake these sweet, rich loaves to give away, wrapped in foil and tied with red or green ribbon. Make some for the family, too.

1 orange
1 cup coarsely chopped cranberries
1 large egg
2 cups all-purpose flour
½ teaspoon salt
1½ teaspoons baking powder
½ teaspoon baking soda
1 cup sugar
2 tablespoons (1 ounce) cold butter,
   cut into small pieces
1 cup chopped pecans or walnuts

Heat the oven to 350 degrees. Lightly butter a 9-by-5-inch loaf pan.

Scrape the colored rind from the orange and toss it with the cranberries. Squeeze the juice into a measuring cup and add enough water to make ¾ cup. Beat the egg and add it to the juice.

Stir together the flour, salt, baking powder, baking soda and sugar in a large bowl. Cut the butter into the dry ingredients, mixing with your fingertips or 2 knives until crumbly. Pour the juice into the dry ingredients and stir just to combine. Gently fold in the cranberries and nuts. Turn the batter into the prepared pan.

Bake for 45 to 50 minutes or until a toothpick inserted in the center of the loaf comes out clean. Let the loaf cool for 10 minutes in the pan set on a wire rack and then turn the loaf out onto the rack to cool completely.

Chop chilled cranberries in the bowl of a food processor fitted with the metal chopping blade. Add a little flour (to prevent them sticking together) and process just until coarsely chopped.

Autumn Pear Bread

Makes one 9-by-5-inch loaf

When the pears are ripe and plentiful in the fall, use them as often as you can. Their delicious flavor only comes once a year (although spring Bartletts are nearly as good as the fall ones). Baking the finest pears you can find into this sweet loaf with a buttery streusel topping is one of the best ways we know to spend an autumn afternoon—and to enjoy this fabulous fruit to the full.

2¹/₂ cups all-purpose flour
1 teaspoon salt
2 teaspoons baking soda
2 teaspoons cinnamon
¹/₂ teaspoon ground nutmeg
¹/₂ teaspoon powdered ginger
8 tablespoons (4 ounces) butter, at room
*   temperature*
1 cup sugar
2 large eggs, at room temperature
1 pound firm, ripe pears, coarsely chopped,
*   approximately 3 or 4 pears*

TOPPING:
6 tablespoons flour
6 tablespoons sugar
4 tablespoons (2 ounces) butter
1 tablespoons grated lemon rind

Heat the oven to 350 degrees. Lightly butter a 9-by-5-inch loaf pan.

Stir together the flour, salt, baking soda, cinnamon, nutmeg and ginger. In another bowl beat the butter until light and fluffy. Gradually beat in the sugar and then the eggs, one at a time. When the mixture is smooth, add the pear pieces and mix well. Stir the dry ingredients into the batter and pour into the prepared pan.

Mix the topping ingredients together until crumbly. Sprinkle the topping evenly over the batter.

Bake for 1 hour and 15 minutes or until a toothpick inserted in the center of the bread comes out clean. Cool the loaf in the pan on a wire rack for 10 minutes and then turn out onto the rack to cool completely.

Jamaican Banana Bread

Makes one 9-by-5-inch loaf

Raisins and dark rum combine in a classic quick bread that is one of the best around. Banana bread is superb toasted and spread with butter in the morning, sliced and served with tea in the afternoon or nibbled on late at night while watching an old movie on television.

1 pound very ripe bananas, 3 to 4 medium-size bananas
1 teaspoon dark rum
²/₃ cup golden raisins
2 cups all-purpose flour
8 tablespoons (4 ounces) butter, softened
¹/₂ cup sugar
1 large egg, at room temperature
1 tablespoon baking powder
¹/₂ teaspoon salt
¹/₂ teaspoon ground nutmeg
1 tablespoon grated orange rind
¹/₂ cup finely chopped pecans

When selecting bananas for baking, choose large, fragrant, very ripe specimens with darkly speckled skin.

(continued)

Heat the oven to 350 degrees. Lightly butter a 9-by-5-inch loaf pan.

Mash the bananas in a bowl with a fork and add the rum. In another bowl toss the raisins with 2 tablespoons of the flour.

Cream the butter with the sugar until fluffy and light. Add the egg and beat until smooth.

In another bowl sift the remaining flour with the baking powder, salt and nutmeg. Add the grated orange rind. Make a well in the center of the flour mixture and add half the banana mixture, blending well, and then half the butter mixture. Repeat the process with the rest of the bananas and the remaining butter mixture. Stir in the raisins and nuts. Scrape the batter into the prepared pan.

Bake for 1 hour until the loaf is lightly browned and a toothpick inserted in the center comes out clean. Remove the pan to a wire rack. Cool for 10 minutes before removing the bread from the pan. Cool completely on the rack.

CHAPTER 5

COFFEE CAKES

An old-fashioned country weekend breakfast would not be complete without a freshly baked coffee cake. Nor would a contemporary city brunch, no matter how sleek the tableware and streamlined the food. Coffee cakes are as much a part of the morning meal as eggs and bacon, pancakes and sausage, freshly squeezed orange juice and strong, creamy coffee. Generously flavored with cinnamon, nuts, fruit or berries, their pleasing sweetness and crumbly textures complement breakfast fare of every description.

All the recipes that follow are for coffee cakes raised with baking powder and baking soda. This means that they are simple to mix up the same morning they are to be served—no need to let them rise for hours before baking as with yeast doughs. These coffee cakes come in many shapes and sizes; some are studded with raisins, cranberries or nuts; some are topped with sweet crumbly streusels or slices of fruit. Several, we hope, will become treasured in your family to be served on holidays and special Sundays when breakfast is a most memorable meal.

Sunday-Morning Raisin Loaf

Makes one 9-by-5-inch loaf

Toast a slice of this orange-scented raisin bread, spread it with sweet butter or perhaps cream cheese—and then sit back, pour another cup of coffee and enjoy the Sunday paper.

> ³⁄₄ *cup orange juice*
> *1 cup raisins*
> *4 tablespoons (2 ounces) butter*
> *1 tablespoon grated orange rind*
> *2 large eggs, at room temperature*
> ³⁄₄ *cup sugar*
> *1 teaspoon vanilla extract*
> *2 cups all-purpose flour*
> *1 teaspoon baking powder*
> ¹⁄₂ *teaspoon baking soda*
> ¹⁄₂ *teaspoon salt*
> ¹⁄₂ *cup chopped walnuts*

Heat the oven to 325 degrees. Lightly butter a 9-by-5-inch loaf pan.

Heat the orange juice until it is almost boiling. Put the raisins, butter and orange rind in a bowl and pour the orange juice over them. Set aside to cool.

In another bowl beat the eggs with the sugar until thick. Add the vanilla and stir into the raisin mixture. In another bowl sift together the flour, baking powder, baking soda, and salt. Add to the raisin mixture and stir just until moistened. Fold in the walnuts. Lightly spoon the batter into the loaf pan.

Bake for about 1 hour until the loaf is golden brown and a toothpick inserted in the center comes out clean. Remove the loaf to a wire rack. Cool for 10 minutes before removing the loaf from the pan. Cool completely on the rack.

Chocolate Swirl Coffee Cake

Makes 1 large bundt cake

Similar to a marble cake, this sweet coffee cake baked in a bundt pan will satisfy any cravings you might have for chocolate in the morning.

>1 cup (8 ounces) butter, softened
>1 1/2 cups sugar
>3 large eggs, separated, at room temperature
>1 teaspoon vanilla extract
>1/2 teaspoon almond extract
>2 1/2 cups all-purpose flour
>2 teaspoons baking powder
>1/4 teaspoon salt
>1 cup sour cream, at room temperature
>1/4 cup unsweetened cocoa
>1 teaspoon cinnamon
>3 tablespoons hot coffee

Heat the oven to 350 degrees. Butter a 12-cup bundt pan and dust with flour.

Cream the butter in a bowl with 1 1/4 cups of the sugar until fluffy. Add the egg yolks one at a time, beating until smooth after each addition. Beat in the vanilla and almond extracts.

In another bowl sift together the flour, baking powder and salt. Add a third of the flour mixture to the butter mixture, stirring just to combine, then stir in a third of the sour cream. Repeat the process to add in the rest of the flour mixture and the rest of the sour cream.

Mix the cocoa and cinnamon in a small bowl. Add the coffee slowly, stirring until smooth. Remove half the batter to another bowl. Add the cocoa mixture to the remaining batter and mix until smooth.

Beat the egg whites until they form soft peaks. Beat

Bundt pans are tube pans with molded sides. If you do not have one, use a straight-sided tube pan instead, the sort of pan you use to bake angel food cake.

in the remaining ¼ cup sugar until the whites are stiff. Divide the whites between the chocolate and plain batters and fold in gently.

Using a large spoon, place alternating spoonfuls of the batters in the pan, continuing until both batters are used up. Spread each spoonful of batter in the pan with the back of the spoon. Finally, tap the pan gently but firmly on the counter to settle the batter.

Bake for about 1 hour until a toothpick inserted in the center of the pan comes out clean. Remove the pan to a wire rack and let the cake cool in the pan for 10 minutes. Remove the cake from the pan and cool completely on the rack.

Cinnamon Crumbcake

Makes one 9-inch cake

The next time you have a group of friends in for coffee, make this ever-so-easy crumbly cake, crowned with a buttery cinnamon topping.

TOPPING:
4 tablespoons (2 ounces) butter, softened
⅓ cup firmly packed brown sugar
2 tablespoons sugar
1 cup graham cracker crumbs, approximately
    12 crackers
½ teaspoon cinnamon

CRUMBCAKE:
8 tablespoons (4 ounces) butter
¾ cup sugar

1 large egg, at room temperature
1/2 teaspoon vanilla extract
1 cup all-purpose flour
1 teaspoon baking powder
1/4 teaspoon salt
1 cup buttermilk, at room temperature

Heat the oven to 375 degrees. Butter a 9-inch cake pan and dust with flour.

Make the topping in a bowl by combining the butter, sugars, graham cracker crumbs and cinnamon. Work the mixture with your fingertips until it resembles coarse meal. Set aside until ready to use.

In another bowl beat the butter with the sugar until light and creamy. Beat in the egg and the vanilla extract. Sift together the flour, baking powder and salt and add half the dry ingredients to the butter mixture, followed by half the buttermilk. Repeat the process with the rest of the dry ingredients, then the rest of the buttermilk, making a smooth batter. Spread the batter evenly in the prepared pan and sprinkle with the reserved topping.

Bake for 30 to 40 minutes until a toothpick inserted in the center comes out clean. Remove to a wire rack and cool for 10 minutes before removing the cake from the pan. Serve warm.

50

MUFFINS & QUICK
BREADS

Apple Pecan Spice Coffee Cake

Makes one 9-inch tube cake

A seductively spicy, nut-filled coffee cake for sophisticated taste buds.

BROWN SUGAR-PECAN MIXTURE:
3/4 cup packed brown sugar
1/4 cup all-purpose flour
1 teaspoon cinnamon
1/4 teaspoon ground cloves
1/8 teaspoon powdered ginger
1/8 teaspoon ground nutmeg
4 tablespoons (2 ounces) butter, chilled and cut
    into 1/2-inch pieces
1 cup chopped pecans

CAKE:
12 tablespoons (6 ounces) butter, softened
1 1/2 cups sugar
3 large eggs, at room temperature
2 teaspoons vanilla extract
3 cups all-purpose flour
2 teaspoons baking powder
1 teaspoon baking soda
3/4 teaspoon salt
1 cup sour cream, at room temperature
1 1/2 cups loosely packed grated tart apples,
    1 to 2 medium-size apples

Heat the oven to 350 degrees. Lightly butter and flour a 9-inch tube pan.

Stir together the brown sugar, flour, cinnamon, cloves, ginger and nutmeg. With a pastry blender or 2 knives, cut the butter pieces into the sugar mixture until it resembles coarse meal. Stir in the pecans.

Cream the butter and sugar together until light. Add the eggs one at a time, beating well after each addition. Beat in the vanilla. In another bowl stir together the flour, baking powder, baking soda and salt. First, add half the sour cream, then half the flour mixture into the butter mixture, beating just until combined. Repeat the process with the rest of the sour cream, then the remaining flour mixture. Stir in the apples.

Turn half the batter into the prepared pan and sprinkle the surface evenly with half the brown sugar-pecan mixture. Top with the remaining batter, smoothing its surface. Sprinkle the rest of the brown sugar mixture over the top.

Bake for 85 to 95 minutes until a toothpick inserted into the center of the coffee cake comes out clean. Remove the pan to a wire rack. Cool for 20 minutes in the pan before removing the cake from the pan. Cool completely on the rack. This cake freezes well.

BAKING WITH APPLES

Look for firm, tart specimens when baking with apples. Experiment with those grown locally in your region and remember that flavor, not beauty, is the most important criterion for baking apples.

Orange Blossom Bundt Cake

Makes 1 large bundt cake

A handsome bundt cake is always a welcome sight on the morning table, whether you are putting together a weekend meal for the family or a holiday brunch for good friends. Subtle flavors of oranges, ginger and cloves make this one especially good.

1 cup (8 ounces) butter, softened
1 1/2 cups sugar
2 large eggs, at room temperature
3 egg whites
1 1/2 teaspoons grated orange rind
1 teaspoon vanilla extract
2 3/4 cups all-purpose flour
1/2 teaspoon baking soda
1/2 teaspoon cinnamon
1/4 teaspoon ground nutmeg
1/4 teaspoon powdered ginger
1/8 teaspoon ground cloves
1 1/4 cups buttermilk, at room temperature
1 tablespoon confectioners' sugar

Heat the oven to 350 degrees. Lightly butter a 12-cup bundt pan.

Beat together the butter and sugar until fluffy. Add the eggs and egg whites one at a time, beating well after each addition. Beat in the orange rind and vanilla. In another bowl sift together the flour, baking soda, cinnamon, nutmeg, ginger and cloves. Add half the flour mixture to the butter mixture, stirring just to combine, then add half the buttermilk. Repeat the process, adding first the rest of the flour mixture, then the rest of the buttermilk. Turn the batter into the prepared pan.

Bake for 40 to 45 minutes until a toothpick inserted

into the center of the cake comes out clean. Remove the pan to a wire rack and cool for 15 minutes before removing the cake from the pan. Cool completely on the rack and serve sprinkled with the confectioners' sugar.

Maple Apple Coffee Cake

Makes one 9-inch single-layer cake

Bring the good flavors of New England into your kitchen with this simple coffee cake sweetened with maple syrup and topped with cinnamon-dusted slices of tart apples. If you cannot find maple syrup, substitute honey thinned with a little apple cider.

8 tablespoons (4 ounces) butter, softened
3 large eggs, at room temperature
3/4 cup maple syrup
2 teaspoons vanilla extract
1 cup all-purpose flour
1 cup whole wheat flour
2 teaspoons baking powder
1/8 teaspoon salt
1 teaspoon cinnamon
1/4 teaspoon ground nutmeg

TOPPING:
3 to 4 medium-size tart, firm apples, peeled,
  cored and sliced, to make 3 to 4 cups
2 tablespoons (1 ounce) butter
4 tablespoons sugar
1/2 teaspoon cinnamon

(continued)

Heat the oven to 350 degrees. Butter a 9-by-2-inch round cake pan.

Beat the butter until light. Add the eggs one at a time, beating well after each addition. Beat in the maple syrup gradually until the mixture is light. Add the vanilla. In another bowl sift together the flours, baking powder, salt, cinnamon and nutmeg. Fold the dry ingredients into the butter mixture. Spoon the batter into the prepared pan.

To make the topping, put the apples in a bowl and toss with the butter, sugar and cinnamon. Arrange decoratively on top of the batter. Bake for 40 to 45 minutes until the apples are browned and tender and a toothpick inserted in the center of the cake comes out clean. Remove the cake to a wire rack and let cool for 10 minutes before removing it from the pan. Serve warm.

MAPLE SYRUP

Pure maple syrup is made in the late winter and early spring when the days are beginning to warm up but the nights are still cold. This is when the sap runs most freely in the trees of New England and the Great Lakes states, where most sugar maples grow. The lightest colored, most delicate tasting syrup is graded "A" and sometimes called "fancy." Unhappily, pollution and pesis are causing some sugar maples to die and the supply of maple syrup is dwindling.

CHAPTER 6

TEA CAKES

The classic afternoon tea, so much a part of drawing-room comedies of the 1920s and 1930s, may be something of a relic. Rarely do we have the leisure or opportunity to gather in a drawing room filled with overstuffed, chintz-covered chairs grouped around a large fireplace where the logs always burn with merry flames. In this scenario, a low table near the fire is set with a large tray laden with teapots, china and platters of cakes and sweets. More than likely, today's tea time consists of a mug of good, strong tea and a slice of cake taken at the kitchen table while the late afternoon sun slants through the window.

But afternoon tea is one tradition that is finding its way back into fashion. Increasingly, we are using late afternoon as a time to relax with a few friends over a nice cup of properly brewed tea and a plateful of scrumptious tea cakes. This chapter has some of the best: classic recipes for scones and shortbread; new ideas such as apple date nut cake; and homey old gingerbread and nut cakes. Isn't it about time to put the kettle on?

Scones

Makes 8 scones

Scones, the British cousins of baking powder biscuits, are tender and fluffy, although denser. Traditionally served for tea in Britain and elsewhere with butter and preserves, often homemade, scones are frequently offered with a topping of thick clotted (Devonshire) cream as well. You could substitute crème fraîche or stiffly whipped cream, or just rely on butter. Simply smashing, anyway.

Scones can also be cut into rounds, like biscuits. The rather sticky dough may seem hard to work at first, but you will quickly get the knack.

> *2 cups all-purpose flour*
> *4 tablespoons sugar*
> *1/2 teaspoon salt*
> *2 teaspoons baking powder*
> *6 tablespoons (3 ounces) butter*
> *2 eggs*
> *1/3 cup cream or sour cream*
> *1/4 teaspoon vanilla extract*

Heat the oven to 375 degrees. Lightly butter a baking sheet.

Sift the flour in a bowl with the sugar, salt and baking powder. Add the butter and work with your fingertips until the mixture resembles coarse meal.

Combine the eggs, cream and vanilla in a bowl and beat until combined. Add to the flour mixture and stir just until moistened.

Flour your hands well. Working quickly, lightly pat the dough into an 8-inch round. With a sharp knife, score the round into 8 wedges.

Set it on the baking sheet and bake for about 20 minutes until the top is browned and a toothpick inserted in the center comes out clean. Remove the round of scones to a wire rack and cool for a few minutes. Cut along the score marks and serve warm.

Poppy Seed Bread

Makes one 9-by-5-inch loaf

Poppy seeds give this sweet loaf a distinct flavor and crunchy texture. Both seem to go as well with a nice cup of tea as any sort of quick bread.

> *8 tablespoons (4 ounces) butter*
> *¾ cup sugar*
> *3 large eggs, separated*
> *1 teaspoon vanilla extract*
> *1 cup all-purpose flour*
> *1 teaspoon baking powder*
> *⅛ teaspoon salt*
> *½ cup milk or yogurt*
> *½ cup poppy seeds*

Heat the oven to 350 degrees. Butter a 9-by-5-inch loaf pan.

Beat the butter with the sugar until light and creamy. Beat in the egg yolks and vanilla.

Sift together the flour, baking powder and salt. Add half the flour mixture to the butter mixture, stirring until smooth, then add half the milk. Repeat the process with the rest of the flour mixture and the rest of the milk. Stir in the poppy seeds.

Beat the egg whites until stiff and fold into the batter. Turn the batter into the prepared pan. Bake about 45 minutes until the cake is browned and the top springs back when lightly touched.

Eccles Cakes

Makes 10 cakes

As often as not, when it is tea time in England, these little currant-filled packets of sweet pastry will be on the tray. Understandably, they are a national favorite.

FILLING:
2 tablespoons (1 ounce) butter, melted
3 tablespoons sugar
1/2 cup currants
1 tablespoon chopped candied ginger
1 teaspoon grated lemon rind
1/8 teaspoon ground allspice
1/8 teaspoon ground nutmeg

SHORTCRUST PASTRY:
2 cups all-purpose flour
1/2 teaspoon salt
1 teaspoon sugar
6 tablespoons (3 ounces) butter, chilled
3 tablespoons (1 1/2 ounces) vegetable shortening
3 to 4 tablespoons cold water
1 egg yolk
3 tablespoons cold milk

Combine the butter, sugar, currants, ginger, lemon rind, allspice and nutmeg in a bowl. Mix well and set aside.

In another bowl sift together the flour, salt and sugar. With your fingertips, work in the butter and vegetable shortening until they are the size of peas. Add the water and toss until the dough holds together. Shape the dough into a disk and chill for 1 hour before using.

Heat the oven to 475 degrees.

Roll the dough out on a floured work surface into a

sheet ¼ inch thick. Cut out ten 3-inch rounds with a biscuit cutter or a glass dipped in flour. Gather the scraps, dusting off any excess flour, and reroll as necessary to make the full number of rounds.

Put a tablespoon of the currant mixture in the center of each pastry round. Draw up the edges and pinch them together to seal the pastry. Flatten lightly until the currants can be seen through the pastry. Place the cakes seam side down on a baking sheet.

Make a glaze by beating the egg yolk with the milk in a small bowl and brush it lightly over the rounds. Cut a cross on the top of each and bake for about 15 minutes until the pastry is golden. Serve warm or at room temperature.

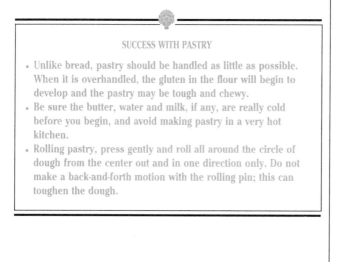

SUCCESS WITH PASTRY

- Unlike bread, pastry should be handled as little as possible. When it is overhandled, the gluten in the flour will begin to develop and the pastry may be tough and chewy.
- Be sure the butter, water and milk, if any, are really cold before you begin, and avoid making pastry in a very hot kitchen.
- Rolling pastry, press gently and roll all around the circle of dough from the center out and in one direction only. Do not make a back-and-forth motion with the rolling pin; this can toughen the dough.

Shortbread

Makes 8 to 10 wedges

Many a cook has quickly patted out a round of sweet, crumbly shortbread in preparation for afternoon tea. Soft and buttery, the wedges are best served while still warm.

> 1 cup (8 ounces) butter, softened
> 1 cup confectioners' sugar
> 1/2 teaspoon vanilla extract
> 2 cups all-purpose flour
> 1/4 teaspoon salt
> 2 tablespoons sugar

Heat the oven to 325 degrees.

Beat the butter with the confectioners' sugar until light and creamy. Add the vanilla and beat well.

Sift together the flour and salt and fold into the butter mixture.

Put the dough on an unbuttered baking sheet and pat into a circle 3/8 inch thick. Score into 8 or 10 wedges with a sharp knife. Mark the edge decoratively with a fork.

Bake for 25 minutes until the shortbread is pale brown around the edges. Remove the shortbread to a rack and let cool for 10 minutes. Sprinkle the sugar on top and cut the shortbread into wedges.

Nut Cake

Makes one 8-inch cake

An old-fashioned nut cake needs no more embellishment than a dusting of confectioners' sugar before it is sliced and put on the tea table.

> *8 tablespoons (4 ounces) butter, softened*
> *3/4 cup sugar*
> *2 large eggs*
> *1 teaspoon vanilla extract*
> *1 3/4 cups all-purpose flour*
> *1/2 teaspoon baking powder*
> *1/2 teaspoon salt*
> *1/2 cup milk*
> *1 1/2 cups chopped walnuts*
> *Confectioners' sugar*

The accepted rule is a teaspoonful of loose tea for every cup and then another good one for the pot. Be sure to warm the teapot with hot water before starting to brew tea, and always use boiling hot water.

Heat the oven to 350 degrees. Butter an 8-inch cake pan and dust with flour.

Cream the butter and sugar until light and fluffy. Add the eggs one at a time, beating well after each addition. Stir in the vanilla.

Sift together the flour, baking powder and salt. Stir half the flour mixture into the butter mixture until the batter is smooth, then stir in half the milk. Repeat the process with the rest of the flour mixture and the remaining milk. Fold in the walnuts and turn the batter into the prepared pan.

Bake the cake for about 45 minutes until a toothpick inserted in the center comes out clean. Remove the cake to a wire rack to cool in the pan for about 10 minutes before removing it to cool completely. Dust with confectioners' sugar before serving.

Gingerbread

Makes one 9-inch cake

Using fresh ginger gives this tender bread an intense flavor and pungent aroma. You may find it becoming your very favorite gingerbread recipe.

When grating fresh ginger, always remove the fibrous pieces that accumulate on the grater. If you prefer to grate the ginger in a food processor, chop it very fine before processing.

8 tablespoons (4 ounces) butter, softened
1/2 cup packed brown sugar
1/4 cup molasses
1/4 cup maple syrup
2 large eggs
3 tablespoons finely grated fresh ginger
1 1/2 cups all-purpose flour
1 teaspoon baking soda
1/2 teaspoon cinnamon
1/4 teaspoon ground nutmeg
1/8 teaspoon ground cloves
1/8 teaspoon black pepper
1/2 cup buttermilk or yogurt

Heat the oven to 350 degrees. Lightly butter a 9-inch cake pan and dust with flour.

Beat the butter with the brown sugar until light. Beat in the molasses and maple syrup. Add the eggs one at a time, beating well after each addition. Stir in the ginger.

Sift together the flour, baking soda, cinnamon, nutmeg, cloves and pepper. Add half the dry ingredients to the butter mixture, mixing until smooth, then stir in half the buttermilk. Repeat the process with the rest of the dry ingredients and the remaining milk. Pour the batter into the prepared pan.

Bake for 30 to 40 minutes until a toothpick inserted in the center comes out clean. Cut into squares and serve warm with whipped cream or ice cream.

Apple Date Nut Cake

Makes one 9-inch cake

This heavy, full-flavored tea cake is sure to hit the spot on cold, raw afternoons when you yearn for a warm hearth, a hot cup of tea and a substantial piece of fruit-filled cake.

> *1 cup whole wheat flour*
> *1 cup all-purpose flour*
> *1 teaspoon baking soda*
> *1 teaspoon cinnamon*
> *1/2 teaspoon salt*
> *1/2 cup vegetable oil*
> *1 cup packed light brown sugar*
> *2 large eggs*
> *2 medium-size apples, peeled, cored and chopped, about 2 cups*
> *1 cup chopped walnuts*
> *3/4 cup chopped dates*

Heat the oven to 350 degrees. Lightly butter and flour a 9-inch-square baking pan.

Stir together the flours, baking soda, cinnamon and salt. In another bowl beat the oil and brown sugar together until blended. Add the eggs one at a time, beating well after each addition. Beat in the flour mixture. Stir in the apples, walnuts and dates. The batter will be very stiff. Scrape it into the prepared pan.

Bake for 35 to 40 minutes until a toothpick inserted in the center comes out clean. Remove the pan to a wire rack to cool for about 10 minutes, then turn the cake out onto the rack to cool completely. Cut into squares and serve.

CHAPTER 7

HEALTHY MUFFINS & HEARTY BREADS

Baked goods tend to be thought of as great-tasting treats which are not too good for us. Made with butter, sugar, eggs, chocolate and other calorie- and fat-laden confections, their place in our hearts lies all too heavily on our consciences.

Get rid of the guilt and start baking! In this chapter are recipes for tasty, rich, scrumptious muffins and quick breads that will meet your every craving while adding the minimum fat and cholesterol to your diet.

These recipes rely on low-fat yogurt and skim milk for richness and moisture. They use egg whites whenever possible, excluding the egg yolks, and employ nonstick vegetable spray for greasing the pans to cut down even further on calories. Packed with nutritious grains, fruits and vegetables, they will permit you to indulge in a homemade muffin or slice of bread without regret. You might even want to pack a few in your backpack for your next strenuous hike or bike ride through the park.

Healthy Bran Muffins

Makes 16 mini muffins

Unprocessed bran and skim milk increase the health-fulness and reduce the calories in these robust mini muffins. Tuck two (no, *three*) in your briefcase or brown bag.

> 1 1/2 cups unprocessed bran
> 1/2 cup boiling water
> 1 cup all-purpose flour
> 1 tablespoon baking powder
> 1/8 teaspoon salt
> 3/4 cup skim milk, at room temperature
> 1/4 cup molasses
> 1 large egg, at room temperature
> 2 tablespons vegetable oil
> 1 teaspoon vanilla extract
> 1/2 cup chopped dates

Toss sticky dried fruit such as dates with a little flour to keep the pieces from sticking to the knife as you chop. Dried fruits are also more manageable when they are chilled.

Heat the oven to 400 degrees. Spray sixteen 2-by-1 3/16-inch (3 tablespoon) muffin cups with nonstick vegetable cooking spray.

Stir together the bran and boiling water and let stand at least 2 minutes. In another bowl stir together the flour, baking powder and salt. In a separate bowl combine the milk, molasses, egg, oil and vanilla, then stir in the bran mixture. Make a well in the center of the dry ingredients, add the milk mixture and stir just to combine. Stir in the dates. Spoon the batter into the prepared muffin cups.

Bake for 15 to 20 minutes until a toothpick inserted in the center of one muffin comes out clean. Remove the tin(s) to a wire rack. Cool for 5 minutes, then remove the muffins from the cups and finish cooling them on the rack. Serve warm or completely cool.

Oat Bran Muffins

Makes 10 muffins

These slightly sweet muffins are bursting with healthy good flavor. The yogurt makes them especially tender and moist. As an extra bonus, they freeze beautifully.

Health professionals report that oat bran seems to help lower blood cholesterol. Remember that it is the egg yolk that contains cholesterol, not the egg white.

2 cups oat bran
1/4 cup packed brown sugar
2 teaspoons baking powder
1/2 teaspoon baking soda
1/8 teaspoon salt
1 cup plain low-fat yogurt, at room temperature
1/4 cup molasses
2 large egg whites, at room temperature
2 tablespoons vegetable oil
1 teaspoon vanilla extract
1/4 cup currants

Heat the oven to 400 degrees. Spray ten $2^5/8$-by-$1^1/8$-inch (6 tablespoon) muffin cups with nonstick vegetable cooking spray. Fill any unused cups with water.

Stir together the oat bran, sugar, baking powder, baking soda and salt. In another bowl stir together the yogurt, molasses, egg whites, oil and vanilla. Make a well in the center of the oat bran mixture, add the yogurt mixture and stir just to combine. Stir in the currants. Spoon the batter into the prepared muffin cups.

Bake for 15 to 20 minutes until a toothpick inserted in the center of one muffin comes out clean. Remove the tin(s) to a wire rack. Cool for 5 minutes before removing the muffins from the cups and finish cooling on the rack. Serve warm or cool completely.

Sunflower Raisin Muffins

Makes 10 muffins

Sunflower seeds, available at most health food stores, imbue these raisin-studded muffins with a gentle crunch and delightful flavor.

> *1 cup all-purpose flour*
> *1 cup whole wheat flour*
> *1/3 cup packed brown sugar*
> *1 1/2 teaspoons baking powder*
> *1/8 teaspoon salt*
> *3/4 cup skim milk, at room temperature*
> *3 tablespoons vegetable oil*
> *1 large egg, at room temperature*
> *1 teaspoon vanilla extract*
> *1 cup raisins*
> *1/2 cup shelled sunflower seeds*

Heat the oven to 400 degrees. Spray ten $2^5/_8$-by-$1^1/_8$-inch (6 tablespoon) muffin cups with nonstick vegetable cooking spray. Fill any unused cups with water.

Stir together the flours, sugar, baking powder and salt. In another bowl stir together the milk, oil, egg and vanilla. Make a well in the center of the flour mixture, add the milk mixture and stir just to combine. Stir in the raisins and sunflower seeds. Spoon the batter into the prepared muffin cups.

Bake for 15 to 20 minutes until a toothpick inserted in the center of one muffin comes out clean. Remove the tin(s) to a wire rack. Cool for 5 minutes, then remove the muffins from the cups and finish cooling them on the rack. Serve warm or cool completely.

Apple Spice
Whole Wheat Muffins

Makes 9 muffins

There is very little fat in these chunky, fruit-filled muffins, yet they taste sinfully rich. The apples, which make them moist, are highlighted by the good flavors of cinnamon, cloves, nutmeg and ginger.

Keep whole wheat flour in the refrigerator. Seal it well so that it does not absorb odors from other chilled foods.

1 cup whole wheat flour
1 cup all-purpose flour
1/3 cup packed brown sugar
2 teaspoons baking powder
1/2 teaspoon baking soda
1 teaspoon cinnamon
1/8 teaspoon ground cloves
1/8 teaspoon ground nutmeg
1/8 teaspoon powdered ginger
1/8 teaspoon salt
1 cup buttermilk, at room temperature
1 large egg, at room temperature
2 tablespoons vegetable oil
1 1/2 teaspoons vanilla extract
1 large tart green apple, peeled, cored and cut
    into 1/4-inch pieces, approximately 1 cup

Heat the oven to 400 degrees. Spray ten 2 5/8-by-1 1/8-inch (6 tablespoon) muffin cups with nonstick vegetable cooking spray. Fill any unused cups with water.

Stir together the flours, sugar, baking powder, baking soda, spices and salt. In another bowl stir together the buttermilk, egg, oil and vanilla. Make a well in the center of the flour mixture, add the buttermilk mixture and stir just to combine. Stir in the apple. Spoon the batter into the prepared muffin cups.

Bake for 15 to 20 minutes until a toothpick inserted

in the center of one muffin comes out clean. Remove the tin(s) to a wire rack. Cool for 5 minutes before removing the muffins from the cups. Serve them warm or cool completely on the rack.

Vegetable Corn Bread

Makes one 8-by-4-inch loaf

Several good handfuls of corn kernels, scallions, carrots and green peppers combine to make this a substantial, fresh-tasting loaf. Serve it with grilled chicken and a lightly dressed tomato salad. Or pack a slice with your lunchtime apple and yogurt.

1 cup yellow cornmeal

1 cup all-purpose flour

2 1/2 teaspoons baking powder

1/2 teaspoon baking soda

1/8 teaspoon salt

1 cup buttermilk, at room temperature

1 large egg plus 1 large egg white, at room temperature

2 tablespoons vegetable oil

1/4 teaspoon Tabasco sauce

8 3/4-ounce can whole kernel corn with no added salt, drained, approximately 1 cup

1/4 cup sliced scallion

1/4 cup grated carrot

1/4 cup chopped green pepper

(continued)

Heat the oven to 400 degrees. Spray an 8⅜-by-4⅜-by-2⅝-inch loaf pan with nonstick vegetable cooking spray.

Stir together the cornmeal, flour, baking powder, baking soda and salt. In another bowl stir together the buttermilk, egg and egg white, oil and Tabasco. Make a well in the center of the cornmeal mixture, add the buttermilk mixture and stir just to combine. Stir in the corn, scallion, carrot and green pepper. Turn the batter into the prepared pan and smooth the top.

Bake for 30 to 35 minutes until a toothpick inserted in the center comes out clean. Remove the pan to a wire rack. Cool for 10 minutes, then remove the bread from the pan and finish cooling it on the rack. Cool completely before serving or wrapping in transparent wrap and foil for freezing.

Carrot Yogurt Loaf

Makes one 8-by-4-inch loaf

Dark and moist, this carrot loaf satisfies a sweet tooth without being terribly sweet.

1 cup whole wheat flour
1 cup all-purpose flour
⅓ cup packed brown sugar
2 teaspoons baking powder
½ teaspoon baking soda
⅛ teaspoon salt
¼ teaspoon cinnamon
Pinch ground nutmeg

*½ cup plain low-fat yogurt, at room
     temperature*
1 large egg, at room temperature
2 tablespoons vegetable oil
1 teaspoon vanilla extract
1 cup grated carrot
½ cup golden raisins

Heat the oven to 400 degrees. Spray an 8⅜-by-4⅜-by-2⅝-inch loaf pan with nonstick vegetable cooking spray.

Stir together the flours, sugar, baking powder, baking soda, salt, cinnamon and nutmeg. In another bowl stir together the yogurt, egg, oil and vanilla. Make a well in the center of the flour mixture, add the yogurt mixture and stir just to combine. Stir in the carrot and raisins. Turn the batter into the prepared pan and smooth the top.

Bake for 30 to 35 minutes until a toothpick inserted in the center comes out clean. Remove the pan to a wire rack. Cool for 10 minutes, then remove the bread from the pan and finish cooling it on the rack. Cool completely before serving or wrapping in transparent wrap and foil for freezing.

CHAPTER 8

SPREADS FOR BREADS

There is more to muffins and quick breads than the baking. There is the very important business of eating. Break open a freshly made biscuit and breathe in the rich aroma; break off a small piece and savor it on your tongue. Wonderful, isn't it? Now, spread a bit of creamy sweet butter on the muffin and try it again. Even better, we'll wager. How about some peach butter or strawberry jam? What about sweetened cream cheese or butter laced with luscious golden honey? Mmmm....

Setting the table with pretty porcelain bowls and sparkling glass jars filled with composed butters and homemade jams is a way to heighten the pleasure of the meal. Everyone likes to experiment with condiments and spreads, which add a new dimension to their favorite muffin or slice of bread.

Refrigerator Strawberry Jam

Makes 1 pint

In this easy recipe for chunky strawberry jam, the
partly cooked berries are lifted from the syrup and then
added back, after the syrup has cooked and thickened.
We have found that this results in especially bright
colored, fresh tasting jam. The jam is a little less sweet
than a strawberry preserve, and will not keep for as
long, either. It lasts very well for two to three weeks in
the refrigerator, however, and is absolutely wonderful
spread on fresh, hot muffins.

> *2 heaping pints fresh strawberries*
> *1 cup sugar*
> *2 teaspoons lemon juice*

When you rinse
strawberries (and
all fruit) to rid
them of any
pesticide residue,
do not let the
berries soak in
water or even sit
under running
water for more
than a few
seconds. They
may absorb water
and lose flavor.

Wash and hull the strawberries and drain well. Quar-
ter the berries and layer them with the sugar in a 2-
quart enamel or stainless steel pot. Allow the mixture
to stand for several hours or overnight until the berries
have exuded their juice.

Bring the mixture to the boil over moderate heat,
stirring gently until the sugar is dissolved. Allow the
mixture to boil rapidly, skimming the white froth as it
rises to the surface. Add the lemon juice and continue
to boil the jam until the syrup begins to thicken. Remove the berries with a slotted spoon and reserve them
in a bowl. Boil the syrup over high heat for 5 to 8
minutes until it is thick enough to fall from a spoon in
sheets. Return the berries to the syrup and cook for a
few minutes longer. Remove the pan from the heat.
When the mixture is cool, spoon it into a container, seal
tightly and store in the refrigerator.

Peaches and Sweet Cream Spread

Makes about 1³⁄₄ cups

A smooth, nutty spread, lightly flavored with sweet peach schnapps, this is delicious when lavishly slathered on oatmeal raisin muffins or thick slices of banana bread.

> *8-ounce package cream cheese, softened*
> *³⁄₄ cup ground blanched almonds*
> *¹⁄₂ cup chopped, pitted dates*
> *¹⁄₄ cup peach schnapps*
> *¹⁄₈ teaspoon powdered ginger*

Combine all the ingredients in a medium-sized bowl and blend until smooth. Cover and chill for several hours to give the flavors time to blend.

Cream Cheese Vanilla Spread

Makes 1 cup

Vary the flavor of this sweetened cream cheese spread by substituting almond extract for the vanilla. If you like the taste of rum or cognac, add a few teaspoons instead of the extract. The spread is delectable on nut cake, berry-filled muffins and most coffee cakes.

> *8-ounce package cream cheese, softened*
> *2 tablespoons (1 ounce) lightly salted butter*

¹/₄ cup confectioners' sugar
¹/₂ teaspoon vanilla extract
¹/₈ teaspoon ground nutmeg (optional)
1 to 2 tablespoons milk or cream

Combine all the ingredients in a bowl, adding enough milk to make a creamy consistency. Cover the bowl and chill to give the flavors time to blend. Serve at room temperature for the best flavor and consistency.

Crème Fraîche

Makes about 1 cup

A rich, creamy topping with a mild but discernible tang, crème fraîche is good to have on hand for luxuriously lazy weekend breakfasts, tea time and dessert. Spoon it over warm muffins, coffee cakes, scones or sweet quick breads. If you prefer it a little sweeter, add a pinch of confectioners' sugar just before serving. It keeps for a week or so.

1 cup heavy cream
2 tablespoons cultured buttermilk

Stir the cream and buttermilk together in a glass or ceramic bowl. Cover the bowl loosely and let it stand in a warm place for 12 to 24 hours until the contents have thickened. Stir the crème fraîche, cover and chill until ready to use.

If possible, buy heavy cream that is not ultra-pasteurized. It is sometimes hard to find and you may have to try a local dairy, but the flavor is worth the search.

Spiced Peach Butter

Makes 2 cups

Peach butter keeps for a week or two in a tightly sealed container in the refrigerator. You will be glad you made a couple of cups of it, because once this highly flavorful, sweet condiment becomes a familiar item on the breakfast table, it will not last long.

10 large fresh peaches, about 4 pounds
Juice of 2 lemons
1/2 teaspoon cinnamon
1/8 teaspoon ground cloves
1/8 teaspoon ground nutmeg
Sugar

Wash, pit and peel the peaches and cut them into chunks. Process the peaches in a food processor or blender until coarsely chopped. (You will have the best success if you do this in several batches of 3 or 4 peaches.)

Combine the peaches, lemon juice, cinnamon, cloves and nutmeg in a large, heavy saucepan. Simmer for 1 to 2 hours, stirring frequently, until the mixture is quite thick. Remove the peach butter from the heat and sweeten to taste with sugar. Stir the sugar into the hot butter to dissolve it completely.

SOFTENING IN THE MICROWAVE

It is easy to soften butter and cream cheese in the microwave. Make sure any foil wrapping is removed, put the butter or cheese on a microwavable dish, cover with transparent wrap or wax paper and set at Medium (50 percent power) for 25 to 50 seconds. Repeat for 10 seconds or so if the butter or cheese is not sufficiently soft.

Lemon-Orange Butter

Makes ¹/₄ cup

For a dash of sweet-sour citrus zip, try this easy, quick butter on your breakfast muffin.

> *4 tablespoons (2 ounces) butter, softened*
> *¹/₄ teaspoon sugar*
> *¹/₈ teaspoon grated lemon rind*
> *¹/₄ teaspoon grated orange rind*

Mix all the ingredients together in a small bowl. Use the butter right away or cover the bowl and chill in the refrigerator. Bring it out a little ahead of serving to give it time to soften slightly.

Honey Butter

Makes ¹/₂ cup

We have all made our own version of honey butter by spooning golden honey on top of the butter already melting into a hot muffin. This recipe produces the same effect with one smooth spreading.

> *8 tablespoons (4 ounces) lightly salted butter,*
> *softened*
> *2 tablespoons honey*
> *1 teaspoon lemon juice*

Beat the butter in a small bowl until creamy. Add the honey and lemon juice and mix well. Use the butter right away or chill it in a covered bowl.

Herb Butter

Makes ¼ cup

We have combined the flavors of oregano, thyme and basil, but certainly encourage you to experiment with your own favorite herbs. Dried herbs are usually more readily available than fresh, so we have used them here, but by all means make herb butter with fresh herbs if you have them in your garden or find them in the market. When using fresh, you will need about twice the amount of herb, but again, experiment on your own. Herb butter tastes great with corn muffins and quick breads that are not too sweet.

4 tablespoons (2 ounces) butter, softened
⅛ teaspoon dried oregano, crumbled
⅛ teaspoon dried thyme, crumbled
⅛ teaspoon dried basil, crumbled

Mix all the ingredients together thoroughly in a small bowl. Cover and chill to give the flavors time to blend. Let the butter soften slightly before serving.

For best flavor, crumble dry herbs between your fingertips or in your cupped palm. The heat of your body releases the herbs' oils and good flavor.

INDEX